Quick and Easy Staple Recipes for a Gypsy Life

BENA GREY

Quick and Easy Staple Recipes for a Gypsy Life

Concoctions to help you make a fantastic meal in a pinch, for a few or many!

Copyright © 2017 Bena Grey
All rights reserved.

No portion of this book may be reproduced – mechanically, electronically, or by any other means, including photocopying – without written permission of the author.

Author: Bena Grey

Printed In The United States Of America
1st printing [December 2017]

ISBN: 1981812555

ISBN-13: 978-1981812554

DEDICATION

To all my fellow travelers, a meal without wine is just breakfast. Enjoy each meal and the people who are with you as you make memories, living life to the fullest each day.

One's destination is never a place, but a new way of seeing things.
- Henry Miller

CONTENTS

	Acknowledgments	i
1	Appetizers and Breads	Pg 3
2	Breakfast	Pg 9
3	Desserts	Pg 13
4	Entrées	Pg 16
5	Mixtures and Miscellaneous	Pg 21
6	BONUS – Slushy Ice Bag	Pg 32

ACKNOWLEDGMENTS

This would not have been possible without my gypsy mother and her wanderlust that took us through many unique adventures and experiences. Allowing us to cook up a variety of concoctions to feed a few and many; making memories and enjoying the little things as we made memories.

This book is only a few recipes in each area because they are very versatile and can be used to make many dishes at the spur of the moment. The purpose for this initial book is to give you critical foundational recipes to add to your cooking arsenal. Helping you be amazing and whip up phenomenal meals at a moment's notice allowing you to focus on making memories – enjoying the moments of your life.

CHAPTER 1 APPETIZERS AND BREADS

BEEF JERKY

Ingredients:

1 pound of Lean Round or Flank Steak

- Remove all fat and place the meat in the freezer. When the meat is semi-frozen it is easily cut into 3/8 to 1/4 inch strips. The thinner the slices the faster the drying.

- Cut against the grain for tender, or with the grain if you prefer chewy beef jerky.

Ingredients for Marinade:

4 Tablespoons of Soy Sauce

4 Tablespoons of Worcestershire Sauce

1 Tablespoon Ketchup

1/4 teaspoon Black Pepper (add more if you like to spice it up)

1/4 teaspoon Garlic Powder

1/4 teaspoon Onion Salt

1/2 teaspoon Salt

DIRECTIONS:

1. Marinade works best if done overnight but can be done with as little as 1 hour.

2. Take meat out of marinade and place on cookie sheets, do not overlap.

3. Place the jerky in a 200 degree Fahrenheit oven. Leave the door cracked open.

4. Dry jerky in the oven for 8 to 10 hours or more. It's ready when it bends like a green willow without breaking.

5. Long term storage should be in the refrigerator. Easily double the recipe.

REFRIGERATOR CUCUMBERS

Ingredients to put in Mixing Bowl:

    8 Cups Sliced Unpeeled Cucumbers

    1 Medium Sliced Onion

    2 teaspoon Salt

    1 Cup Vinegar

    2 Cups Sugar

Ingredients to put in Cheesecloth/Spice Bag:

    1 teaspoon Celery Seed

    1 teaspoon Dill Seed

    1 Heaping teaspoon Pickling Spice

DIRECTIONS:

1. Put Cucumbers and Onion's in bowl.

2. Place spice bag ingredients in cheesecloth bag and tie. Lay in bowl.

3. Mix Salt, Vinegar, and Sugar together well then pour over ingredients in the bowl.

4. Store in refrigerator. Will keep indefinitely.

SPINACH ARTICHOKE DIP

INGREDIENTS:

1 Can Artichokes - drained and chopped (may use artichoke hearts)

1 Cup Fresh Spinach - chopped

1 Cup Hellmans' Mayonnaise

1/2 teaspoon Minced Garlic

1/2 teaspoon Black Pepper

1 Cup Parmesan Cheese

1/2 Cup Cream Cheese

DIRECTIONS:

1. Preheat oven to 400 degrees Fahrenheit.
2. Mix all ingredients into a baking dish.
3. Bake at 400 degrees Fahrenheit for 8-10 minutes.
4. Serve with bread or crostini's.

BANNOCK

Ingredients:

    4 Cups Flour

    1/2 Cup Vegetable Oil or Shortening

    1/4 Cup Sugar

    1 1/2 Cup Milk

    4 rounded teaspoon Baking Powder

    1/4 teaspoon Salt

DIRECTIONS:

1. Blend dry ingredients together.
2. Mix in vegetable oil/shortening and milk with dry ingredients.
3. Knead together well.
4. Drop in biscuit size shapes into cast iron skillet.
5. Bake on slow fire. Turn over once.

Serves 8

For 1 Serving:

    1 Cup Flour

    1 teaspoon Baking Powder

    1/8 teaspoon Salt

    Milk and Shortening to thick consistency

BRAN MUFFINS

Ingredients:

1/2 Cup Cracklin' Oat Bran Cereal

1 Cup All-Bran Cereal

3/4 Cup Sugar

1/4 Cup Butter

1 1/4 teaspoon Baking Soda

1/4 teaspoon Salt

1/2 Cup Boiling Water

1 Egg

1 1/4 Cup Flour

1 Cup Milk

DIRECTIONS:

1. Put all ingredients in a bowl and mix together. It will be a bit chunky.

2. Can put in microwave muffin tin to make individual muffins at will.

3. Goo stores for 6 weeks in the fridge.

4. Bake at 400 degrees Fahrenheit for 15-20 minutes or 15 minutes in an individual pie maker with a tinfoil strip across the bottom to ease pulling muffin out.

Makes 11 Large Muffins

MAPLE SYRUP

Ingredients:

    1/2 Cup Sugar

    1/2 Cup Brown Sugar

    1/2 Cup Water

    1/4 teaspoon Maple Flavoring

DIRECTIONS:

1. Boil together sugars and water.

2. Once mixed well, add flavoring

3. Use immediately. Store in fridge and warm up prior to use.

OVERNIGHT OATMEAL

INGREDIENTS:

1 Cup Steel Cut Oatmeal

1 Cup Chopped Apple (may substitute Apple Sauce)

1/2 Cup Raisins (may substitute Cran-raisens)

1/2 teaspoon Cinnamon

1/4 teaspoon Salt

1 Tablespoon Melted Butter

1/4 Cup Brown Sugar

2 Cups Milk

Optional: 1/2 Cup Chopped Walnuts

*Best prepared right before going to bed so it will be ready for breakfast.

DIRECTIONS:

1. Spray slow cooker with non-stick spray.

2. Put all ingredients inside slow cooker and mix together.

3. Place slow cooker on low.

4. By morning it will be ready to eat.

5. First thing in the morning, stir oatmeal and decide if you need to add more milk for consistency.

Serves 4 portions. Double or triple recipe for large groups.

EGG CUPS W/HOLLANDAISE SAUCE

Ingredients for Egg Cups:

- 12 Large Eggs
- Cooked Bacon - Diced
- Pre-made Pie Crust
- Kosher Salt
- Fresh Ground Pepper

Ingredients for Hollandaise Sauce:

- 3 Large Egg Yolks
- 3 teaspoons White Vinegar
- 1/4 teaspoon of Cayenne Pepper (optional)
- 2 1/4 Sticks of Melted Butter
- 1/2 teaspoon Salt

Ingredients for Toppings:

- 3 Scallions Diced
- 3 Tablespoons Shredded or Grated Cheese (to taste)

DIRECTIONS:

1. Preheat oven to 350degrees Fahrenheit.

2. Spray muffin tin with non-stick spray.

3. Take a round cookie cutter and cut circles of pie crust. Place one in bottom of each pre-greased muffin tin cup.

4. Place diced bacon pieces in each muffin tin cup.

5. Crack egg into each muffin tin cup. Sprinkle with salt and pepper to taste.

6. Bake in oven 15-20 minutes at 350degrees Fahrenheit. Next, while eggs are baking, make Hollandaise Sauce.

7. Put yolks, vinegar and cayenne pepper in the blender. Pulse a few times to mix together.

8. Melt butter in microwave. With blender running, gradually add in the melted butter.

9. If sauce seems too thick, slowly add in warm water - up to 1 teaspoon.

10. To serve - Use a thin spatula or knife to run around the edge of each muffin tin cup and gently pop each egg portion out. Serve immediately with hollandaise sauce, scallions, and cheese.

Serves 12 single portions.

BISCUITS AND GRAVY

INGREDIENTS:

1 pound Sage Pork Sausage

1 medium Chopped Onion

6 Tablespoons Flour

1 Quart Milk (4 Cups)

1/2 teaspoon Poultry Seasoning

1/2 teaspoon Ground Nutmeg

1/4 teaspoon Salt

Dash of Worcestershire sauce

Roll of Buttermilk Biscuits

DIRECTIONS:

1. Put sausage and onion into pan, cooking until sausage browned.

2. Simultaneously, put biscuits on cookie sheet and bake according to directions.

3. In pan with sausage and onions, add in flour and stir. The mixture will clump up. It's okay. Cook until it bubbles and brown, about 5 minutes.

4. Next, add in milk. Stir well.

5. Add in all seasonings and the Worcestershire sauce. Cook, constantly stirring until thickened to right consistency.

6. Place biscuit on plate and pour sausage gravy over, then eat.

3 CHAPTER DESSERTS

CHOCOLATEY CAKE

Ingredients:

1 Package Chocolate Cake Mix (moist preferred)

1 small Package Instant Chocolate Pudding

4 Eggs

1 1/4 Cup Water

1/2 Cup Vegetable Oil

12oz. Package Chocolate Chips or whatever you'd like

Non-Stick Bundt Pan

DIRECTIONS:

1. Mix all ingredients together until moistened.

2. Fold in Chocolate chips or item of choosing.

3. Spray bundt pan with non-stick spray or coat with butter.

4. Pour mixture into 13x9 pan or Bundt pan.

5. Bake at 350 degrees Fahrenheit for 45 minutes (13x9 pan) or 1 hour (bundt pan).

6. If using bundt pan, turn out immediately onto serving plate to cool.

EASY-PEASY CHOCOLATE CHIP COOKIES

Ingredients:

    1 Box White or Yellow Cake mix (moist preferred, not butter)

    2 Eggs

    1/2 Cup Oil

    2 Tablespoon Water

    6 oz. Chocolate Chips

DIRECTIONS:

1. Mix all ingredients together well.

2. Using two spoons place blobs on cookie sheet.

3. Bake at 350 degree's Farenheit for 13 minutes.

** Very soft and chewy

NO BAKE FUDGE COOKIES

Ingredients:

    1/2 Cup Milk

    2 Cups Sugar

    1 stick of Butter

    5 Tablespoons Cocoa Powder

    1/2 Cup Peanut Butter

    1 Tablespoon Vanilla

    3 Cups Quick Oats

    Wax paper

DIRECTIONS:

1. Bring milk, butter, sugar, cocoa power to a boil for 3 minutes.
2. Add peanut butter and vanilla. Stir.
3. Mix in Quick Oats well.
4. Drop onto wax paper, placed on a cookie sheet or tray.
5. Place in refrigerator or freezer to set.

Optional: add raisins, nuts, or trail mix.

4 CHAPTER ENTRÉES

EASY TURKEY

INGREDIENTS:

1 Turkey - Size/Weight doesn't matter

1 Stick of Butter

Seasoning or Dry Rub of Choice

DIRECTIONS:

1. Put two inches of water in bottom of the turkey roaster pan.

2. Season turkey and dot with butter.

3. Place in roasting pan, cover with tinfoil.

4. Bake in oven at 150 or 200 degrees Fahrenheit for 12 hours. Example: 9pm to 9am.

5. Last 30 minutes take off tinfoil to allow browning and crisping of the skin on the turkey.

Very moist and tender turkey! Cook stuffing separately and not in this turkey.

ITALIAN SAUSAGE

INGREDIENTS:

5 pounds Coarse Ground Pork butt

1 Tablespoon Coarse Ground Black Pepper

1 Tablespoon Salt

1 teaspoon Anise Seed

6 Cloves pressed Garlic

1 Tablespoon Fennel Seeds

1 Cup Chilled Red Wine or Ice Water

Casing for sausage

DIRECTIONS:

1. Mix all ingredients together thoroughly.

2. Stuff the mixture into a casing.

3. Now broil under medium heat, pan fry, or use how you'd like.

ROAST CHICKEN

INGREDIENTS:

    5 pounds Whole Chicken

    Olive Oil

    Herbed Chicken Spice Mix or Herbs d' Provence

    8oz. Of a Beverage (Wine, Beer, Juice or Broth)

    4 Diced Potatoes

    2 Diced Carrots

    1 Chopped medium Onion

    1 Cup of any other vegetables diced you'd like

Use either a clay chicken roasting pot with the tube in the middle OR use a normal pan and place a ramekin or oven worthy cup in the center with the liquid.

DIRECTIONS:

1. Rub outside of chicken with olive oil and favorite spice mixture.

2. Make sure to get some in the cavity.

3. Fill the ramekin or center tube with liquid.

4. Place the chicken on the cylinder, standing upright. Add vegetables to the bottom around the chicken.

5. Place an additional little bit of liquid on the base of the pot.

6. Preheat oven to 450 degrees Farenheit. Cook chicken 10-15 minutes.

7. Then reduce temperature to 350 degrees Farenheit.

8. Roast 20minutes per pound. 1 1/2 hours for 4 1/2 pound Chicken.

SPICY CHILI

INGREDIENTS:

5 teaspoons of Spicy Chili Seasoning Mix

1 pound Beef, cut into 1 inch pieces

2 teaspoon Vegetable Oil

1 pound Lean Ground Beef

1 medium Onion, chopped

1 can (28oz.) Diced Tomatoes, undrained

2 cans (15oz. each) Kidney Beans or choice of beans for Chili

DIRECTIONS:

1. Heat oil and lightly brown beef cubes.
2. Add 3 teaspoons Chili seasoning mix, toss to coat while browning.
3. Add ground beef and brown with beef cubes.
4. Toss in onion, cook until tender.
5. Add tomatoes, and 2 more teaspoons Spicy Chili Seasoning Mix.
6. Stir in chili beans.
7. Cook on low for 30 to 40 minutes or until meat is tender.

Yields: 10 servings (2 1/2 quarts) per batch

VENISON SAUSAGE

INGREDIENTS:

1 pound Fine Ground Bacon

4 pounds Coarse Ground Venison Meat

2 Tablespoon Sugar

1 Tablespoon Salt

1 Tablespoon Sage

1 teaspoon Coriander

1 teaspoon Allspice

1 1/2 teaspoon Mustard Seed

8 Cloves of pressed Garlic

2 Tablespoon Black Pepper

1 teaspoon Marjoram

1 Cup cold water OR Red Wine

Casing for sausage

DIRECTIONS:

1. Mix all ingredients together thoroughly.

2. Stuff the mixture into a casing.

3. Now cook, bake, fry or use how you'd like.

5 CHAPTER MIXTURES AND MISCELLANEOUS

ADOBO SEASONING MIX

INGREDIENTS:

1 Tablespoon Lemon Pepper Seasoning

1 Tablespoon Garlic Powder

1 Tablespoon Onion Powder or Flakes

1 Tablespoon Dried Oregano

1 Tablespoon Parsley Flakes

1 Tablespoon Achiote Powder (also known as Annatto Seeds)

1/2 Tablespoon Ground Cumin

1 Tablespoon Salt

DIRECTIONS:

1. Combine all ingredients in an airtight container. Mix well.

2. Store in a cool dry place.

3. Delicious on pork chops and other dishes.

Yields: 1/2 Cup

CREAM SOUP MIX

INGREDIENTS:

    2 Cups Instant Nonfat Dry Milk Powder

    3/4 Cup Cornstarch

    1/4 Cup Chicken Bouillon Granules

    1 teaspoon Onion Powder

    1/2 teaspoon Dried Thyme

    1/2 teaspoon Dried Basil

    1/4 teaspoon Black or White Pepper

DIRECTIONS:

1. Combine all ingredients, mix well.
2. Store in airtight container.

USAGE:

1. Blend 1/3 Cup mix and 1 1/4 Cup Water in 1 quart sauce pan until smooth.

2. Bring to a boil for 2 1/2 - 3 minutes. Stirring occasionally.

3. Cool and use as a substitute for one 10 3/4oz. can of condensed cream of chicken, celery or mushroom soup.

4. Optional: For 1 1/2cups of soup blend 1/3 Cup mix and 1 1/2 cup water.

If there's one mixture you add to your cupboard from this book – make it this!

Yields: 3 Cups Dry Mix

DRY ONION MIX

INGREDIENTS:

    1 1/4 Cups Wheat Flour

    1 1/4 teaspoon salt

    1 1/4 teaspoon Onion Powder

    3/4 teaspoon Dry Mustard

    1 teaspoon Paprika

    1 1/4 teaspoon Garlic Powder

    1 1/4 teaspoon Black Pepper

    1 Tablespoon Cajun Spice of your choosing

DIRECTIONS:

1. Sift and mix all ingredients together; adjust spices to suit your taste.

2. Store in airtight container.

1/4 Cup of mixture equals 1 Envelope of Dry Onion Soup Mix

Great in meatloaf, on pot roast, and even biscuits and gravy mix.

FIREWEED HONEY

INGREDIENTS:

50 Pink Clover Blooms

10 White Clover Blooms

18-25 Fireweed Blooms

3/4 teaspoon Alum

5 pound bag of Sugar

3 Cups Boiling Water

Cheesecloth

DIRECTIONS:

1. Rinse the flower blooms in cold water to remove any little critters and bugs.

2. Put all ingredients except the water in the pan, then pour the boiling water over all ingredients and into the pot.

3. Let sit for 10 minutes.

4. Strain through cheesecloth into separate pourable large pot/bowl/container.

5. Put in sterilized canning jars leaving 1/2 inch space at top.

6. Process in a canning water bath for 10 minute before sealing with lids.

HERB BUTTER

INGREDIENTS:

1 pound of Unsalted Butter

1/2 a bunch (4-5 Stems) of Fresh Dill

1/2 a bunch (4-5 Stems) of Fresh Parsley

3-5 Chives

2 Large Cloves of Garlic

Kosher Salt

Optional: Minced Onion

DIRECTIONS:

1. Set butter to the side.

2. Wash the Dill, Chives and Parsley. Dice or chop in a food processor.

3. Dice the garlic or use pre-minced garlic.

4. Mix diced herbs, minced garlic and salt with the butter.

5. Place into containers and store in fridge/freezer OR create a roll using plastic wrap, letting harden in refrigerator. Remove plastic wrap and cut into slices. Repackage and store.

Delicious on steak, pork, and also good on potatoes or vegetables.

ITALIAN AND PIZZA SEASONING

INGREDIENTS:

1 Tablespoon Parsley

1 teaspoon Oregano

1/2 teaspoon Basil

1/4 teaspoon Black Pepper

1 teaspoon Powdered Parmesan Cheese

1/2 teaspoon Powdered Swiss cheese

1/4 teaspoon Powdered Cheddar Cheese

1/2 teaspoon Onion Powder

1 teaspoon Garlic Powder

DIRECTIONS:

1. Mix all ingredients thoroughly in a glass jar.
2. Used old parmesan cheese container to make use easier.

Recommendation: Take cottage cheese, frozen chopped spinach and mix together with this seasoning. Use for Lasagna, Pizza, Calzones, etc...

MARINADE 1 FOR BEEF/PORK

INGREDIENTS:

    1 1/2 Cups Flat Beer of any kind

    1/2 Cup Vegetable Oil

    1 Clove Garlic, Minced

    2 Tablespoons Lemon Juice

    1 Tablespoon Sugar

    1 teaspoon Salt

    3 each Cloves

DIRECTIONS:

1. Mix all ingredients with a whisk.

2. Place in ziploc bag and add beef or pork of choice.

3. Marinade for at least 1 hour before using.

Yields: 2 Cups

MARINADE 2 FOR BEEF/PORK

INGREDIENTS:

1 1/2 Cups Flat Beer of any kind

1/2 teaspoon Salt

1 Tablespoon Dry Mustard

1 teaspoon Ground Ginger

3 Tablespoons Soy Sauce

1/8 teaspoon Hot Pepper Sauce

2 Tablespoons Sugar and Honey mixed together

4 Tablespoons Marmalade

2 Minced Cloves of Garlic

DIRECTIONS:

1. Mix all ingredients with a whisk.

2. Place in ziploc bag and add beef or pork of choice.

3. Marinade for at least 1 hour before using.

Yields: 2 Cups

MARINADE FOR ROUND STEAK

INGREDIENTS:

    1/4 Cup Soy Sauce

    2 Tablespoons Vegetable or Olive Oil

    1/4 Cup Worcestershire Sauce

    1 Tablespoon Lemon Juice

    2 teaspoons Minced Garlic

    1 Tablespoon Ketchup

    1 Tablespoon Mustard

    1/8 teaspoon Black Pepper

    1/2 of a small onion, chopped

DIRECTIONS:

1. Blend well with a whisk.

2. Take 1 - 1inch thick round steak, about 1 1/2 pounds. Poke with fork several times in both sides of meat to tenderize.

3. Put meat in marinade for several hours. Ziploc bag works well.

4. Grill or cook to your desired doneness.

5. Let meat rest for 5 minutes when done cooking, then slice across the grain.

SPICY CHILI SEASONING MIX

INGREDIENTS:

    4 Tablespoons Chili Powder

    2 1/2 teaspoon Ground Coriander

    2 1/2 teaspoon Ground Cumin

    1 1/2 teaspoon Garlic Powder

    1 teaspoon Dried Oregano

    1/2 teaspoon Cayenne Pepper

DIRECTIONS:

1. Combine these ingredients together well.
2. Store in airtight container in a cool place.

Yields: 4 batches (20 teaspoons total)

VERSATILE DRY RUB MIX

INGREDIENTS:

    1/2 Cup Dark Brown Sugar

    1/4 Cup Season Salt (reduce to 1/8 cup for low-sodium version)

    1/4 Cup Hungarian Paprika

    1/4 Cup Smoked Paprika

    1 Tablespoon Garlic Powder

    2 teaspoons Onion Powder

    1 Tablespoon Celery Salt

    2 Tablespoons Chili Powder

    2 Tablespoons Black Pepper

    1 Tablespoon Rubbed Dried Sage

    1 teaspoon Ground Allspice

    1 teaspoon Ground Cumin

    1/4 teaspoon Cayenne

    1/4 teaspoon Ground Mace (alternative is nutmeg)

    1/8 teaspoon Ground Cloves

DIRECTIONS:

1. Use a food processor and mix all the ingredients together.

2. Store in an airtight container or jar.

3. Dry rub is a great gift in a jar, or used on any meat. Delish!

Yields: 1 3/4 Cups

BONUS - SLUSHY ICE BAG

Because you never know when you are going to need one of these!

Ingredients:

    2 each Freezer Ziploc Bags (Gallon Size)

    3 Cups Water

    1 Cup Rubbing Alcohol

DIRECTIONS:

1. Pour Rubbing alcohol and water into one freezer bag and seal with as little air as possible.

2. Put the filled bag inside the other freezer bag and seal.

3. Place in freezer. It will freeze into a moldable slush.

4. Always use a small towel or paper towel around when using.

Always keep a few in the freezer. You never know when this will come in handy.

ABOUT THE AUTHOR

Bena is a traveler who has lived all over North America and over 21 different countries. Heading from place to place based on the intuitive feelings and whims of her gypsy mother. From as far back as she can remember home has been wherever the family is together, location irrelevant. The people make the place.

Printed in Great Britain
by Amazon